Amazing Storms!

by Caroline Hutchinson

D0061424

A powerful storm can bring large ocean waves or dark clouds. Some storms bring both.

▲ thunderstorm

▲ hurricane

Take a look at some powerful storms.
Look for ways that powerful storms
are the same and different.

▲ tornado

What Happens in a Thunderstorm?

A thunderstorm is a powerful storm that starts with a dark cloud. Rain or ice falls. The wind blows, too.

You can see lightning. Lightning heats the air and then you can hear thunder.

The lightning can also start a fire.
The wind is very powerful. Sometimes
it blows so hard that trees fall down.

Most thunderstorms last for about an hour.

▲ You can stay safe. Play a game or read a book inside.

What Happens in a Hurricane?

A hurricane is a powerful storm that starts in the ocean. A hurricane happens when the ocean is warm.

Like in a thunderstorm, rain falls and powerful winds blow. Sometimes the wind blows big waves onto the land.

The center of a hurricane is the eye. The wind is powerful in a hurricane, but the wind is gentle in the eye. Rain does not fall in the eye.

▲ The winds from a hurricane bring the waves onto shore.

A thunderstorm is powerful, but a hurricane is more powerful. A hurricane lasts longer, too. It can last for a week.

▲ You can see the eye of the hurricane.

What Happens in a Tornado?

A tornado is a powerful storm that can start when warm, moist air and cool air meet. The rain falls in a tornado. Powerful winds blow, too.

The wind twists very fast and picks up dirt and dust. A tornado is a dark, tall cloud that can move as fast as a car.

▲ Sometimes we call a tornado a twister.

The wind is so powerful that it can move large things. A tornado sounds like a train is coming!

This powerful storm does not last as long as a thunderstorm or a hurricane. Some tornadoes are only a few minutes long.

▲ Look at this car. A tornado lifted the car off the ground and dropped it here.

A tornado is a powerful storm.
A thunderstorm and a hurricane
are powerful, too. These storms
have some things in common.
They have differences, too!